CONTENTS

C000218976

TOUR OF THE HOUSE

MELBOURNE HALL BEFORE THE CIVIL WAR

Melbourne Hall stands in an idyllic setting at the east end of the village overlooking the 20 acre mill pool. Passers-by get little more than a fleeting glimpse, because its principal aspects are south and east towards the parkland and gardens, while the courtyards and outbuildings separate it from the village to the north and west.

The house has a chequered and unusually well-documented history, and all centuries from the 16th to the 20th have left their mark on the fabric. This, combined with the fact that Melbourne remains a lived-in family home, accounts for its warm, welcoming and comfortable atmosphere. It is now the home of Lord and Lady Ralph Kerr, Lord Ralph being a direct descendant of Sir John Coke who made Melbourne his home in 1629.

Melbourne was a Royal manor until its sale by James I in 1604, and had an unfinished Lancastrian castle built between 1311 and 1322. The castle was demolished in the early 17th century, leaving Melbourne Hall as the most important house in the parish. The Hall was built as a Bishop's palace and its origins can be traced to 1133 when Henry I founded the Bishopric of Carlisle and appointed Adelulf, Prior of Nostell in Yorkshire, as its first bishop. The church and rectory of Melbourne appear to have been granted to Adelulf as part of the original endowment of the bishopric, and Melbourne's outstanding Norman church must have been built either by Adelulf or the King himself.

In the 13th and 14th centuries, successive bishops of Carlisle came to Melbourne as a refuge from the troubled Scottish border, when they used the church as a cathedral and Melbourne Hall as their palace. One particular bishop, Walter Malclerc, had great influence on the development of the village and obtained a royal grant for a yearly fair and a weekly market in 1230. The parish church was never entirely finished, and it was probably Bishop Walter who brought it to a presentable conclusion. He may also have been the first bishop to build a house on the site of Melbourne Hall, a few yards to the east of his church.

By the early 15th century Carlisle was more peaceful. Melbourne was no longer needed as a residence by the bishops, which enabled them to lease their palace and estate there to laymen. Thomas Cromwell, Lord Chancellor of England, took the earliest known lease in

1530 for ten pounds a year. Another eminent lessee was Gilbert Talbot, 7th Earl of Shrewsbury, who took a lease of the rectorial estate at Melbourne in 1589, for the 'yearly and ancient rent' of £45.

These people had houses of their own and unfortunately neglected a clause in their leases that bound them to maintain the house at Melbourne 'with thacking (thatching) and daubing in all things necessary'. In 1595 Sir Francis Needham of London, the current lessee, decided to make his home at Melbourne, but the house and outbuildings were by this time fallen into 'exceeding greate decaye, especially the mansion house which is utterly ruened and not inhabitable withoute great and chardgable reparacions'. John Harpur of Swarkestone and Raphe Sacheverell of Stanton by Bridge, both J.Ps, estimated that more than £200 needed to be spent on the house.

Sir Francis pulled down and rebuilt a large part of it within the next two years. The oldest surviving masonry in the house is probably of this period. The result, known from various plans and documents, was a house with much the same layout as it has today. The principal 'Great Hall' was aligned east-west in the area of the present Dining Room and Study, and there were east and west wings projecting to the south in the place of the present ones. As it does today, the west wing contained the kitchen and sculleries, while the east wing housed the best rooms.

The appearance of the house was, however, very different. The leaded windows had stone mullions and transoms, there were large external chimneystacks and a profusion of gables. The principal front faced south across the pool and was broadly symmetrical with a little court between the wings, closed in by a wall with an elaborate gateway. It was an irregular building that had clearly evolved slowly over time. To our eyes it would no doubt have been very pleasant and quaint, but by the early 18th century it was considered an 'eyesore'.

Sir John Coke

This was the house that confronted Sir John Coke when he purchased Sir Francis Needham's freehold and leasehold estate at Melbourne in 1629 and made it his retirement home. Within a few months of obtaining the lease Sir John had planned substantial alterations, and in November 1629 he wrote out lengthy instructions with measurements and great attention to detail. He divided his directions under separate headings for the masons, carpenters, joiners, smiths, plumbers, glaziers, stonegetters and labourers, plasterers and pargeters, and obtained permission from the Earl of Huntingdon to quarry stone from the foundations of Melbourne Castle, which had been sold away from the Crown in 1604.

The alterations involved rebuilding the north range, including the Great Hall, an extension to the east wing and a new principal staircase there, and various other alterations. The work was all done in an extremely conservative style appropriate to Sir John who has been labelled 'the last Elizabethan'. Sir John ended his directions by ordering the house and its grounds to be measured and plotted, and the plan made as a result still survives. Among the features shown on it are the muniment room (then a dovecot), the important medieval aisled barn that is now part of the Craft Centre, and the compact arrangement of the courtyards and gardens, with hedged alleys, grass plots, a kitchen garden and an orchard.

Sir John's house and grounds were closely hemmed in on all sides by public roads. The road between the hall and the pool was the main highway from Melbourne to Ashby until it was diverted through the present Market Place and High Street in 1788. A steady stream of traffic must have used it to reach the mill, the fields,

and the common, as well as places beyond the parish boundary.

A little lane to the east ran across the middle of the upper parterres of the present garden, and separated the grounds of Melbourne Hall from another large house called Blackwall Hall or the 'nether hall', which was apparently pulled down in the 1630s or '40s.

Sir John's role as Secretary of State to Charles I for eleven years before the Civil War demanded that most of his time was spent in London. For part of this time Melbourne affairs were governed by his son Sir John Coke the Younger (1607-1650), who moved to Melbourne despite the drawbacks pointed out to him by his father. "You shal plant yourself in a town where there are manie beggers, most poore & but a few good livers", he had warned, adding that the local folk would "ingage you into debates and sutes wherin little is to bee gotten but vexation & troble to no end".

On a positive note, Sir John the Younger supervised some much-needed repairs of the parish church, but some of his relationships among the local population were indeed strained, not least those with the Earl of Huntingdon (lord of the manor of Melbourne) and Sir John Harpur of Calke. In 1638, the Cokes enclosed an area of common land called Derby Hills, that was disputed with the Harpurs. An undisciplined mob of Royalist soldiers tore down and burnt the new fences on their way north, apparently encouraged by a £10 bribe from Sir John Harpur. They set fire to the Cokes' new water mill on Derby Hills, and destroyed part of the mill dam. It clearly made no difference that the Cokes were themselves a Royalist family.

It was an ill omen for the future, betraying a civil unrest that was soon to erupt. In 1642 the Civil War broke out and the elder Sir John fled from the advancing Parliamentarians. The younger Sir John stayed until 1648 when he went into exile in France, where he died.

Melbourne Hall as it stands today shows what Sir John's descendants have made of it in more peaceful times. The family surname has changed three times due to inheritance via the female line, and the subsequent story of the house will be related during the tour.

*The Rt. Hon. Thomas Coke
by Michael Dahl.*

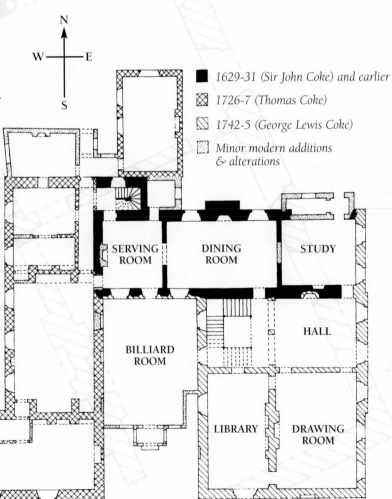

- 1629-31 *(Sir John Coke) and earlier*
- 1726-7 *(Thomas Coke)*
- 1742-5 *(George Lewis Coke)*
- *Minor modern additions
  & alterations*

SERVING ROOM

DINING ROOM

STUDY

HALL

BILLIARD ROOM

LIBRARY

DRAWING ROOM

THE OWNERS OF MELBOURNE HALL

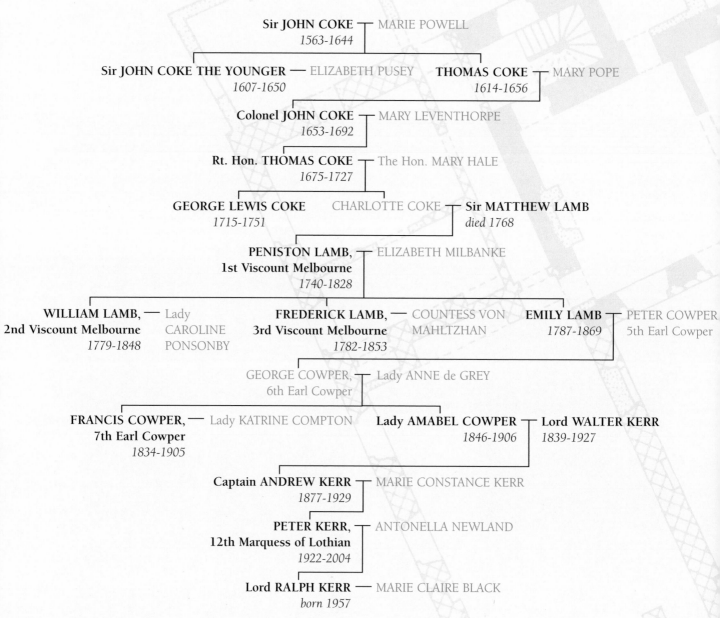

Sir JOHN COKE — MARIE POWELL
1563-1644

Sir JOHN COKE THE YOUNGER — ELIZABETH PUSEY   THOMAS COKE — MARY POPE
1607-1650   *1614-1656*

Colonel JOHN COKE — MARY LEVENTHORPE
1653-1692

Rt. Hon. THOMAS COKE — The Hon. MARY HALE
1675-1727

GEORGE LEWIS COKE   CHARLOTTE COKE — Sir MATTHEW LAMB
1715-1751   *died 1768*

PENISTON LAMB, — ELIZABETH MILBANKE
1st Viscount Melbourne
1740-1828

WILLIAM LAMB, — Lady   FREDERICK LAMB, — COUNTESS VON   EMILY LAMB — PETER COWPER
2nd Viscount Melbourne CAROLINE   **3rd Viscount Melbourne** MAHLTZHAN   *1787-1869* 5th Earl Cowper
1779-1848 PONSONBY   *1782-1853*

GEORGE COWPER, — Lady ANNE de GREY
6th Earl Cowper

FRANCIS COWPER, — Lady KATRINE COMPTON   Lady AMABEL COWPER — Lord WALTER KERR
7th Earl Cowper   *1846-1906*   *1839-1927*
1834-1905

Captain ANDREW KERR — MARIE CONSTANCE KERR
1877-1929

PETER KERR, — ANTONELLA NEWLAND
12th Marquess of Lothian
1922-2004

Lord RALPH KERR — MARIE CLAIRE BLACK
born 1957

Betsy Coke, sister of Thomas Coke

Colonel John Coke and his wife Mary Leventhorpe

William Lamb

Lady Caroline Lamb

Five of the children of Colonel and Mrs. Coke

Rt. Hon. Thomas Coke

Sir John Coke

THE BILLIARD ROOM

The house is entered through the Billiard Room, a conservatory-style addition built in 1911 by Lord Walter Kerr, roofing in the space between the two wings. During the second half of the 19th century, the house and gardens were let out, and the Billiard Room was part of a series of renovations and alterations to the house carried out by Lord Walter after he came to live at Melbourne with his wife Lady Amabel (née Cowper) in 1905.

This Lithograph of the charming Lady Palmerston, hangs in the Serving Room. She was the sister of William Lamb, 2nd Viscount Melbourne.

THE SERVING ROOM

Before the addition of the Billiard Room, the Serving Room was the main entrance to the house. This room, the Dining Room, Study and the rooms above them are the oldest part of the house, substantially altered and partly rebuilt by Sir John Coke in 1629-31. In Sir John's time, the front door led into a traditional 'screens passage' separating the Great Hall (now the Dining Room) from the buttery, which had a staircase down to the cellar. The kitchen was (and still is) beyond the door on the left hand side of the room.

The partition between the buttery and the passage was removed later in the 17th century to form the present room, which has panelling typical of the late 17th or early 18th century. The 'screen' was a partition between the passage and the Dining Room, and the remains of it may still exist in the wall between the Serving and Dining Rooms. Sir John directed that it should be eight feet high or somewhat more, 'handsomly wrought without carving or curious charge', with two doors through it.

The Serving Room furniture: A William IV mahogany table; two cabinets containing Chinese Imari porcelain; some early Derby porcelain on top of the cabinets, made distinctive by the matching ice coolers

THE
DINING ROOM

This is perhaps the only room in the house that Sir John Coke might still recognise as his own. It still measures 30' long, 18' wide and 12' tall as Sir John had designed it, and the fireplace and windows remain in their original positions. The panelling, although much altered, is also original and was stripped of paint in 1907-8, when the elaborate overmantel was imported by Lord Walter Kerr from his Hertfordshire estate.

After the rebuilding of the east wing in 1744, the room lost its former prestige for a time and was demoted to a Games Room complete with a billiard table, battledores and shuttlecocks.

After the Civil War, the younger of Sir John's brother Thomas had to pay £2,200 to the Committee for Compounding in 1655 to regain possession of his Derbyshire estates. He died in the following year, leaving an infant son later known as Colonel John Coke, who went to live at Melbourne Hall with his wife Mary Leventhorpe in 1673. The unfortunate Mrs. Coke bore seven children in eight years and promptly died. She is portrayed with her husband in the attractive double portrait by Sir Peter Lely alongside Sir John's portrait. Colonel Coke raised a troop of horse for the 4th Earl of Devonshire's regiment in the 1688 Revolution. William III later rewarded the Earl by creating him 1st Duke of Devonshire in 1694. The other Lely double shows the Earl and Countess of Chesterfield, whose daughter Mary married Colonel and Mrs. Coke's eldest son Thomas. Their gardens at nearby Bretby were declared in 1705 to be the finest in Europe save for Versailles, and may have provided some inspiration for the Melbourne garden.

Sir John Coke is the man with the large ruff and strikingly perceptive expression who gazes intently into the room from his portrait by the door at the far end. He is seen in his robes of Master of Requests, before his rise to the office of Secretary of State. In Sir John's time, the Great Hall was still the focal point of any large house, and until the Billiard Room was built it was the only link at ground floor level between the two wings of the house. Sir John and his family would have dined in this room, retiring into their private parlours in the east wing while the servants cleared the food and crockery to the kitchens and sculleries in the west wing.

The Dining Room furniture: The room's centrepiece is the George III mahogany dining table with its set of George III mahogany chairs, complete with green leather cushions. In the Dining Room are fourteen 17th century walnut chairs with high backs. Four of these are of the time of Charles II and the others are from the William and Mary period. They have 20th century tapestry seats worked by members of the family. A fine George I walnut side table with Derbyshire alabaster top; an interesting oak table coaster or cheese board given as a present by Queen Victoria and Prince Albert to Lord Melbourne.

In the Dining Room hangs this attractive double portrait by Sir Peter Lely of Colonel John Coke and his wife Mary Leventhorpe in 1673. The unfortunate Mrs. Coke bore seven children in eight years and promptly died. Colonel Coke raised a troop of horse for the 4th Earl of Devonshire's regiment in the 1688 Revolution. William III later rewarded the Earl by creating him 1st Duke of Devonshire in 1694.

14

THE STAIRCASE HALL

16

The Hall is dominated by three large Leventhorpe family portraits. These are said to have been brought to Melbourne from the Leventhorpe family home at Sawbridgeworth in Hertfordshire by Mary Leventhorpe upon her marriage to Colonel John Coke in 1673.

The difference in character between the Dining Room and the Hall is immediately obvious, the Hall and the rooms beyond being built in 1742-5 for George Lewis Coke, the last of the Melbourne Cokes. The oak staircase with carved tread ends and three balusters per tread is a particularly fine feature. At the top of the stairwell is the only ornate plaster ceiling in the house. According to tradition, the plasterers were set to work on this while they were waiting for less refined work elsewhere in the building.

In the hall hangs this mid 19th century overmantel mirror in rococo style with sconces and a portrait of Lady Amabel Kerr (née Cowper) as a young girl.

At the top of the stairs is a large portrait of five of the children of Colonel and Mrs. Coke, painted by Jacob Huysmans in 1680. A son Francis died shortly before the portrait was done and a daughter had died the previous year. She is reputed to be the cherub at the top, looking down on her brothers and sisters. It is a fashionable pastoral portrait, set in an Arcadian landscape, and an important example of its kind. Thomas Coke (1675-1727) who inherited the house in 1696, stands on the right. He became Vice Chamberlain to Queen Anne and George I, and therefore spent the greater part of this time in London, where he had a house in St. James's Place.

THE STAIRCASE HALL

Betsy Coke, sister of Thomas Coke

At Melbourne, it was Thomas's unmarried sister Elizabeth ('Betsy'), standing at the other end of the portrait (opposite), who managed his household affairs and cared for Mary and Elizabeth, the two children of Thomas's first marriage. They are pictured, looking rather wooden, in a portrait on the lower landing, and Betsy records the difficulty which Mr. Dahl the painter had in making them sit still. Betsy managed Melbourne very efficiently and corresponded tirelessly with her brother in long, chatty letters that are still a delight to read today. Nothing escaped her notice, and it is partly due to her that we can assemble such a clear and entertaining picture of life at the Hall in the early 18th century.

Her letters record in fine detail the formation of the garden in 1704-5, and the conduct of the staff and workmen. John Sergeant the bailiff was a particularly difficult character. He failed to keep proper accounts, usually claiming that the mice had eaten his papers, and was eventually dismissed. One of Betsy's more frequent complaints was the unsound condition of the house, which had been little altered since 1631 and was beginning to show signs of structural failure. By 1708 it was securely propped, so soundly that Betsy feared it would 'last longer than anyone alive would want it'. Thomas had contemplated the rebuilding of the house since about 1700, but he was undecided on how to proceed, and did not make up his mind until the 1720s. In the meantime he was content to make some modifications to the existing structure, involving alterations to the roofs, new fireplaces and internal fittings and the insertion of newly fashionable double-hung sashes in the garden elevation. He was much more interested in his new garden, and did not turn his attention to the house until it was properly finished round about 1722.

Thomas Coke was concerned that the axis of the garden did not align centrally on the house (as the view from the external door to the garden reveals), due to physical restrictions and the past history of the site. At first he planned to build a new house with its principal facades facing east and west, but the west aspect would have been intolerably cramped by the parish church, the vicarage and the Hall's own outbuildings. By 1725, Coke had reluctantly concluded that the existing layout of the Hall, with fronts facing east and south, made the

The Staircase Hall furniture: A pair of George II tables with marble tops; a late 17th century Dutch marquetry side table; a rare Queen Anne painted pier glass; a set of mid 18th century 'Chinese Chippendale' chairs with caned seats; a clock by Thomas Tempion in a George III case; a late George III oval topped table adapted by Admiral of the Fleet Lord Walter Kerr for use on his flagship.

most advantageous use of the site. Accordingly, he at last resolved to remodel the house by entirely rebuilding the east and west wings, and partially remodelling the remainder.

The west wing was rebuilt first, in 1726, to designs by Francis Smith of Warwick. It is rather conservative for its date and has old fashioned cruciform windows to its west elevation, formerly glazed with lead. The west wing determined the outline that the matching east wing must copy, but Thomas Coke died in 1727 and his only son George Lewis did not come of age until 1736. It was not until 1742 that a messenger was sent 'to Warwick and other places to find Mr. Smith'. Soon after, William Smith was paid ten pounds for 'Journeys & makeing draught & Estimate of Melbourne House', and the building of the east wing was done under

contract by William Jackson for £1500. Most of the work was complete by 1744, which is the date on the fine lead rainwater heads.

The Rt. Hon. Thomas Coke, by Michael Dahl

To make up for the lack of a grand façade to the west, a gatehouse was built at the south end of the stables in 1726 to a drawing by Francis Smith which still survives, based on a draft by Thomas Coke. Every effort was made to persuade Smith to visit Melbourne often. Writing to Thomas Coke in May 1726, the Melbourne agent wrote: 'I would beg of you to write to Mrs. Lillingson (housekeeper at Melbourne) that when Mr. Smith comes that she makes a Bed for him, and treats him Civilly for I must make soe free to acquaint that tho he is a very good natured man yet (a) small thing will disgust him as I am informed and that he will not be willing to lye at any publick house in Melbourne ... he is very much delighted with the Gardens'. The gatehouse has long since disappeared, and stood at the gates to the stableyard immediately east of the church.

George Lewis, the last of the Melbourne Cokes, is shown in the large portrait on the Dining Room side of the stairwell. This painting was done by Antonio David while Mr. Coke was on the Grand Tour, and the Coliseum is shown in the background. George Lewis died a bachelor in 1751 without a male heir; Melbourne therefore passed via his sister Charlotte to his brother-in-law Matthew Lamb, and into a new chapter of its history.

THE STUDY

In the Study the visitor is introduced to the more recent generations of the family. Opposite the fireplace are portraits of Lord Walter Kerr, as Admiral of the Fleet, and Lady Amabel Kerr. Lady Amabel is seen holding a manuscript of the Fiorretti of St. Francis of Assisi which she wrote out and illuminated herself. She was a follower of Cardinal Newman, and the Roman Catholic church in Melbourne was built in her memory by Lord Walter in 1907. On Lady Amabel's death, Melbourne Hall and its Estate passed to the Kerr family through her husband and thence in 1927 to their son Captain Andrew Kerr whose wife, the late Mrs. Andrew Kerr, lived at the Hall for over fifty years after his death. Their son, Peter Kerr, who became the 12th Marquis of Lothian, was brought up at Melbourne and he and his wife Antonella spent the early part of their married life there before moving to the Lothian family home in Scotland. The present owner is their younger son Lord Ralph Kerr who lives at Melbourne with his wife Marie-Claire and their six children. A portrait of Lord Ralph painted by his wife, who is a renowned artist, hangs in the study. Opposite the window there is a portrait of the Marchioness of Lothian by Simon Elwes.

The Study furniture: A William and Mary walnut secretaire; a George III mahogany concertina action card table; an early 19th century plaster gilt over mantel mirror with triple plates; a mid 18th century south German console table with a simulated marble top; a George II carved and gilt mirror.

THE DRAWING ROOM

The Drawing Room is the most formal space in the house. All of its walls were designed to be symmetrical, so there are four doors into it when two would have sufficed. According to tradition the width of the room was contrived especially to accommodate three large portraits of George I, Queen Anne and Prince George of Denmark by Sir Godfrey Kneller, which still remain in the house.

The room was originally built as a Dining Room. It is a long way from the kitchen, but that was not a material consideration in 18th century households well staffed with servants. Its original furnishings included three Egyptian marble slabs with mahogany frames (which together must have formed the dining table), two mirrors between the windows, a dozen mahogany chairs and three sets of yellow damask draw-up curtains.

The Drawing Room furniture: A fine George II breakfront cabinet in the manner of William Kent; a William and Mary side table with a marquetry top; a pair of late George II mirrors; a mid-19th century French boulle bureau of etched brass on tortoiseshell; an early 18th century overmantel mirror.

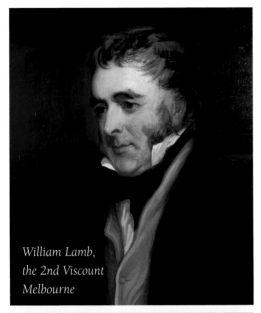

William Lamb, the 2nd Viscount Melbourne

Lady Caroline Lamb, wife of William Lamb, afterwards 2nd Viscount Melbourne

Matthew Lamb's portrait in the Library speaks for itself. The portraits of the Cokes are leisurely and relaxed, but Mathew Lamb is portrayed as the practical, prosaic and matter-of-fact man he was, seated at a desk with his quill pen. Lamb was a *nouveau-riche* lawyer who had been involved with Melbourne in a professional capacity since the 1730s. He married Charlotte Coke in 1740 and a few years later, with the help of a huge legacy of £100,000 left to him by his uncle, he purchased the Brocket Hall Estate in Hertfordshire. Brocket became the main family seat and Melbourne has remained little altered ever since.

The story of William Lamb's disastrous marriage to Lady Caroline Ponsonby is well known. It is easy to understand her attraction for him; her extreme emotions made her an interesting and captivating companion, but her unstable temperament also gave her a vulnerability which made William feel protective towards her. However, her demands on William's time and attention soon became tiresome and of their three children the second was mentally disabled and the other two were stillborn. Caroline's affair with Lord Byron in 1812-13 virtually broke up the marriage. Byron at first found her a fascinating and 'exaggerated woman', but eventually discovered that he had more in common with the solid characteristics of her mother-in-law. Lady Melbourne, manipulative as ever, won Byron's trust and re-directed him towards her equally unsuitable niece Annabella Milbanke, who later become Byron's wife.

A pencil drawing and an etching by Caroline Lamb hang in the Staircase Hall

Caroline's pride did not allow her to accept Byron's rejection; the more she tried to attract his attention, the more violently he reacted.

Shortly before William and Caroline's formal separation in 1825, Caroline was banished from London to Melbourne Hall to spend some time with George and his wife, who had recently gone to live there. Her irritating behaviour was borne patiently. At least she was not outrageous, her misdeeds no worse than walking through the muddy lanes in feathers and thin shoes, and losing her temper with the local children.

George Lamb appeared short, thick, clumsy and uncouth by comparison with William and Frederic, but he was intelligent and good natured with some talent for writing and acting. He lived at Melbourne until his death in 1834, and during this time he built up the basis of the present Library. Meanwhile, William succeeded to the Melbourne title in 1828 and was building up a distinguished political career. He became the young Queen Victoria's personal adviser and confidant, and was her first Prime Minister. He may not have been the best Prime Minister of the century, but he was certainly the most charming.

After Lord Melbourne was defeated by Sir Robert Peel in 1841 and lost the premiership, he stayed at Melbourne on several occasions. His most important contribution to the appearance of the village was the remodelling of the mill pool, visible through the French door in the Library, in 1841-6.

The pool is a picturesque focal point of the village, but has not always been so. In 1701, Thomas Coke found it so 'noisome and unhealthy' to his household that he made arrangements to have it drained completely. This was fortunately never done, partly because of the difficulty in supplying an alternative source of water to the mill, and not least because the pool was soon after used to supply water to the fountains in Coke's new garden.

By the early 19th century the pool was in a dilapidated state, and was silted up completely at the west end. The work of the 1840s involved filling part of it, cleaning out the rest, making the two ornamental islands and landscaping the surrounding area. There can be no doubt today that the pool greatly enhances the setting of the Hall.

William Lamb was succeeded as owner of Melbourne Hall first by his brother Frederic, and then, in 1853 by his sister Emily, now married to Lord Palmerston, her second husband and another of Queen Victoria's Prime Ministers. Lady Palmerston took a great interest in

The Library furniture: A William and Mary cabinet on a stand with barley twist; six Queen Anne chairs with rush seats; a George III mahogany breakfast table crossbanded in satinwood; a George III mahogany bureau; a George II spider leg table.

Melbourne, and Lord Palmerston laid the foundation stone of the Melbourne Athenaeum in Potter Street in 1853. When Lady Palmerston died, Melbourne passed to Francis, 7th Earl Cowper, her grandson by her first marriage.

The 7th Earl had the unusual distinction of being a Prince of the Holy Roman Empire, his forebear the 3rd Earl having been given the honour by the Emperor Joseph II in 1778 with remainder to his heirs male. It is not clear how the 3rd Earl had earned the privilege, but it is possible that his mother may have had an 'attachment' with the Grand Duke of Tuscany, brother of Joseph II and himself a future Holy Roman Emperor, Leopold. The Cowper family seat was at Panshanger near Hertford, and it was not until the 7th Earl's sister Lady Amabel inherited Melbourne as an elderly lady in 1905 that the family returned permanently to the Hall.

It was Matthew and Charlotte's grandchildren by their son Peniston who were the most colourful and interesting generation of the Lamb family. Their characters seem to have been derived more from their mother than their rather nondescript father, who was granted a peerage in 1770 and chose Melbourne as his title. Indeed there was some doubt about how many of the first Lord Melbourne's six children were actually his. It was generally agreed that Peniston the eldest, born in 1770, was his father's son, but it was rumoured that William (later to become the second Lord Melbourne) and Frederick were the sons of Lord Egremont and that George was the son of the Prince of Wales, later George IV.

The first Lady Melbourne was a formidable character from an old Yorkshire family. Although her morals may have been questionable, her beauty, wit and calculating shrewdness earned her widespread respect and admiration, even from people (especially women) who did not like her. By instinct she was socially competitive which sometimes made her appear hard, but her favourite son William remembered her in his old age as 'a remarkable woman, a devoted mother, an excellent wife - but not chaste, not chaste'.

Lady Melbourne, mother of the 2nd and 3rd Viscounts Melbourne

MELBOURNE AND THE WIDER WORLD

Many visitors are surprised to learn that the Australian city of Melbourne takes its name indirectly from Melbourne, Derbyshire.

William Lamb, the 2nd Viscount Melbourne who gave his name to Melbourne, Australia

Melbourne, Australia, was named after Lord Melbourne in 1837, while he was Prime Minister under King William IV; it was previously known as Bearbrass. Another settlement nearby on Hobson Bay was named Williamstown after the King. King William, had he lived long enough, might have been disgruntled to observe that the town named after his Prime Minister flourished, eventually swallowing Williamstown and reducing it to a suburb!

Curiosity has brought Australian tourists to Melbourne, Derbyshire, since at least 1876. That travel across the world is so easy today is due partly to another man

with Melbourne connections – Thomas Cook the travel agent. Cook was born in a humble one-up one-down cottage in Melbourne in 1808 and lived in Melbourne until 1828.

Thomas Cook founder of Thos. Cook & Son Ltd.

Cook's early life in Melbourne was one of hard toil, and he was alarmed to observe that drink not only incapacitated his employers from time to time, but also wasted a good deal of their time and money, preventing their betterment. Cook therefore became an advocate of "temperance", i.e. abstinence from alcohol; his first excursion, on 5th July, 1841, was to transport supporters of a temperance rally from Leicester to Loughborough and back.

Cook always maintained an affection for Melbourne. His birthplace was sadly demolished in 1967, but one of the most significant actions of his last years was the provision of a handsome mission hall and memorial cottages in Melbourne. These, set around a sunken quadrangle on High Street, are still owned and administered by the Trust that Cook set up.

THE GARDENS

The Melbourne garden, with its broad sweeps of lawn, avenues and unexpected vistas, is one of the best known historic gardens in the country and is the best surviving early 18th century English garden in the manner of Le Nôtre. It was never considered ordinary. As early as 1712 it was described as 'curious', and by 1789 it was not only curious but 'old-fashioned' as well.

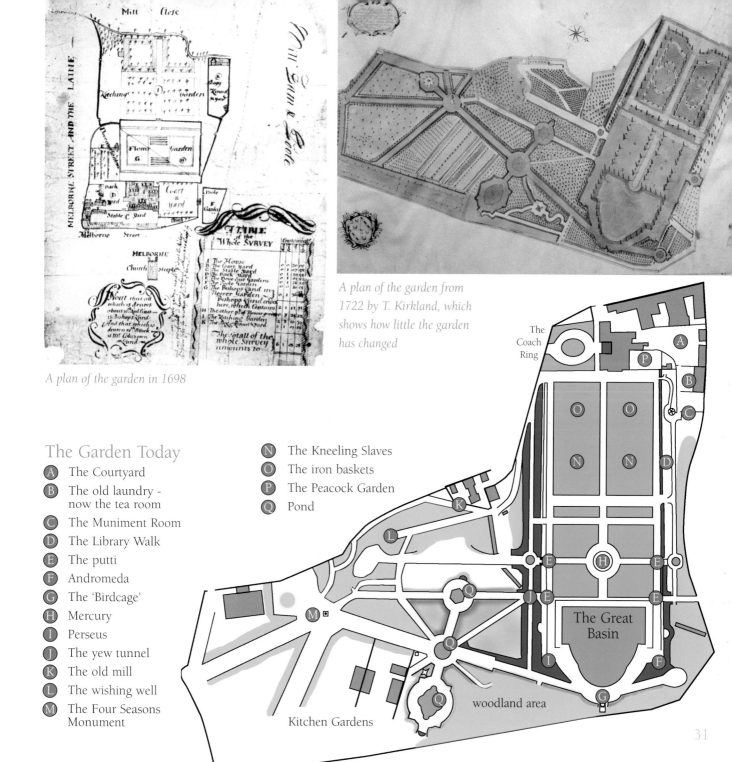

A plan of the garden from
1722 by T. Kirkland, which
shows how little the garden
has changed

A plan of the garden in 1698

The Garden Today

- Ⓐ The Courtyard
- Ⓑ The old laundry - now the tea room
- Ⓒ The Muniment Room
- Ⓓ The Library Walk
- Ⓔ The putti
- Ⓕ Andromeda
- Ⓖ The 'Birdcage'
- Ⓗ Mercury
- Ⓘ Perseus
- Ⓙ The yew tunnel
- Ⓚ The old mill
- Ⓛ The wishing well
- Ⓜ The Four Seasons Monument
- Ⓝ The Kneeling Slaves
- Ⓞ The iron baskets
- Ⓟ The Peacock Garden
- Ⓠ Pond

The Coach Ring

The Great Basin

Kitchen Gardens

woodland area

Documentary evidence shows that Thomas Coke intended to create a new garden at Melbourne as soon as he inherited the house upon his coming of age in 1696. Between 1696 and 1699 large quantities of trees and shrubs were ordered from London and Wise's nurseries at Brompton Park. However, no plans for the enlargement and remodelling of the garden could be implemented at this stage as the house and part of the garden were still held only by lease, and Coke thought it unwise to proceed further without securing the freehold. In 1698 he opened negotiations with the Bishop of Carlisle and a plan of the grounds was made (see page 31), to distinguish the Bishop's land from Thomas Coke's freehold. This plan shows the garden after its enlargement by Sir John Coke the Younger in 1647, and the diagonal line across the flower garden represents (not quite accurately) its former extent. After lengthy deliberation and a period of deadlock, a settlement was reached in 1704 whereby Coke obtained the freehold by Act of Parliament subject to several covenants.

Work on the present garden began immediately. On 6th May 1704 a contract was signed between Thomas Coke and William Cooke of Walcot to reconstruct the old flower and kitchen gardens as 'a division of Partare work' with 'terrasses, sloops, verges and fleets of steps' for £400. By July, Cooke reported that he was ready for the statues, and in October a second contract was agreed with him for laying out the rest of the garden.

Most of this part was entirely new and occupied a former field to the south east of the old garden. This second contract, for £450, comprised levelling and forming the ground for 'divisions of wilderness work', 'reservoirs or bassons for water', fruit walls, kitchen gardens, orchards, plantations and hedged alleys. The moated islands of the 17th century garden were filled in and replaced by the present 'basin' further east.

The Hexagonal Muniment Room, with its attractively-shaped roof, is an important survival from the 17th century garden. Originally a dovecot, it was heightened and remodelled by Thomas Coke in 1708.

The Melbourne garden is often attributed to London and Wise, the royal gardeners, but their chief involvement was as consultants when preliminary plans had already been prepared. The true authors of the garden were William Cooke the contractor and Thomas Coke himself. Perhaps William Cooke has some connection with London's former partner of the same name, and he is surely the same 'Mr. Coke ye Gardainer' who provided plans for a new garden at Calke Abbey in 1709.

THE GARDEN

The important lead statuary was supplied from John Van Nost's workshop in Piccadilly. His account for it is dated 1706, although some of the items appear to have been supplied a few years earlier. It includes '4 pr. of Boyes cast in Mettall £42-00-00, Perseus & Andromeda Do. £45-00-00, an Indian Slave & Black Moor Do. 30-00-00' and, 'a Vause as per Agreement £100-00-00'. All of these can still be found in the garden today. The Indian Slave and the 'BlackMoor' stand in the centres of the parterres next to the house. Perseus and Andromeda stand in the yew hedges to the east of the basin at the bottom of the garden.

The 'Vause' is a large urn known as the 'Four Seasons', which was reputedly a gift from Queen Anne and is the focal point of the south-east part of the garden.

The positioning of the pairs of boys caused Coke a great deal of trouble. At first he proposed to arrange them in military formation on the lawns, but he eventually decided to place them in bays cut out of the yew hedges, where they have remained. Nost also supplied a figure of Mercury after Giambologna which stands on the main axis of the garden to the west of the great basin. The fine stone urns and vases are mostly contemporary and were carved by Watson and Devigne.

Cupid (now lacking his bow and arrow)

Mercury

MELBOURNE HALL

Andromeda,
chained to a rock

The 'Yew Tunnel'

One of the unsung contributors to the Melbourne garden was George Sorocold (born 1668), a pioneer hydraulic engineer who constructed a piped water supply at Derby in 1692. At Melbourne, he was responsible for supplying water to the pools and fountains. He made the fountains work by using direct pressure from the mill pool whose surface lies well above the level of the lower part of the garden.

To give an extra head of water, he raised the level of the pool by two feet, flooding part of the Vicarage garden in the process. Writing to Thomas Coke in 1706, Sorocold says: 'I visited the Parson yesterday who seemed a little uneased about the lower end of his Orchard being under water but upon taking a Pott or two & faire promises to fill up that part with all speed, hee begun your health in a Bumper!'

THE GARDEN

39

In 1710, Cassandra Willoughby of Wollaton noted a visit to Melbourne gardens in her diary: "We went to Mr. Coke's House at Melbourn which stands but ill in a poor Town. The Gardens are very hansome. On one side of the Par Terre Garden is a close walk (*i.e. the present yew tunnel*) which leads to the Wilderness. This walk they told us had been made but 5 years and was then a perfect shade..."

There have been few radical alterations to the gardens since the early 18th century. However, in the earlier part of the 20th century Lord Walter Kerr and his wife Lady Amabel, who inherited Melbourne from her brother, carried out extensive restoration. This included opening up the vista from the house to the Birdcage, which had been obscured by the planting of laurel from south to north across the garden.

In modern times Lord and Lady Ralph Kerr have carried out a programme of maintenance which had been initiated by Lord and Lady Lothian (Lord Ralph Kerr's parents). Lady Ralph Kerr has embarked on an extensive scheme of planting, which includes new beds in the area of the mill stream and bog garden. She has also created a new border along the wall close to the east façade of the house. In addition to this, a large number of interesting new shrubs and trees have been planted at various points around the garden.

Opposite: The crowning feature of the garden is the wrought iron arbour known as 'The Birdcage', which was made by the celebrated ironsmith Robert Bakewell in 1706-8 for £120. It was made at a forge in the basement of 'Stone House', which still stands on the south side of the parish church. Betsy Coke was not fond of Bakewell. During his residence at the Stone House he fathered an illegitimate child and Betsy complained to her brother that his behaviour was not to be borne with. The arbour made Bakewell famous, but its manufacture left him penniless. In form it is derived from wooden arbours common in French gardens. Bakewell went on to produce famous ironwork for many important buildings. Two other examples nearby are the chancel screens in Derby Cathedral and Staunton Harold church.

MELBOURNE HALL

The home of Lord and Lady Ralph Kerr

EARL & COUNTESS OF CHESTERFIELD
(2ND EARL)
SIR PETER LELY

QUEEN,
AND CONSTITUTION